Selected from

Fatherhood

and

Time Flies

BILL COSBY

REVISED EDITION

WRITERS' VOICES

ATTENTION READERS: We would like to hear what
you think about our books. Please send your comments
or suggestions to:

Signal Hill Publications
P.O. Box 131
Syracuse, NY 13210-0131

• • •

SIGNAL HILL™

PUBLICATIONS

Additional material
© 1989 and 1993 Signal Hill Publications
A publishing imprint of Laubach Literacy International

10 9 8 7 6 5 4

First printing: January 1989
Revised Edition: February 1993

ISBN 0-929631-00-5

The words "Writers' Voices" are a trademark of
Signal Hill Publications.

Designed by Paul Davis Studio

Signal Hill is a not-for-profit publisher. The proceeds
from the sale of this book support the national and
international programs of Laubach Literacy.

Acknowledgments

We gratefully acknowledge the generous support of the following foundations and corporations that made the publication of WRITERS' VOICES and NEW WRITERS' VOICES possible: The Booth Ferris Foundation, The Vincent Astor Foundation, and the Scripps Howard Foundation. We also wish to thank Hildy Simmons, Linda L. Gillies, and David Hendin for their assistance.

This book could not have been realized without the kind and generous cooperation of the author, Bill Cosby, and his publisher, Doubleday, a division of Bantam, Doubleday, Dell Publishing Group, Inc. We are also grateful to the William Morris Agency for its help.

Our thanks to Paul Davis Studio and Claudia Bruno, José Conde, Myrna Davis, Paul Davis, and Jeanine Esposito for the inspired design of the books and their covers. We would also like to thank Barbara A. Mancuso of *The New York Times* Pictures for her help with photo research and selection.

Contents

Note to the Reader 6

About the Selections from
    Fatherhood 11

Selected from *Fatherhood*,
    by Bill Cosby 13

About the Selections from
    Time Flies 29

Selected from *Time Flies*,
    by Bill Cosby 31

Questions for the Reader 41

Map of Places Mentioned
    in This Book 46

About Bill Cosby 47

A Timeline for Bill Cosby 58

Resources on Parenting and Aging 59

Note to the Reader

Bill Cosby is one of America's best-loved comic personalities. He also writes funny and honest books. In his book, *Fatherhood,* Cosby writes about what it's like to be a parent. His second book, *Time Flies,* contains his insights about getting older. The *Writers' Voices* book you are reading has short selections from both of these Cosby books.

This series of books is called *Writers' Voices* because every writer has a special voice. The books introduce you to well-known writers and their work. When you're reading this book, try to hear Bill Cosby's writing voice. Think about what makes it special.

ABOUT THIS BOOK

This book has different chapters. The Contents page lists these chapters and the pages where they start.

Bill Cosby's writing is in two chapters: "Selected from *Fatherhood*," starting on page 13, and "Selected from *Time Flies*," starting on page 31.

Reading the other chapters in this book can help you understand Bill Cosby's writing better. You may want to read some of these chapters before reading the selections or after reading the selections.

Here is what these chapters contain:

• The chapters "About the Selections from *Fatherhood*" on page 11 and "About the Selections from *Time Flies*" on page 29 give you a preview of what you will read in Cosby's writing that follows.

• The chapter after the selections called "Questions for the Reader" on page 41 helps you think about what you have read. This chapter has ideas for group discussion and for your own writing.

• The chapter "About Bill Cosby" on page 47 tells you about Bill Cosby's life. Sometimes knowing about a writer's life helps you understand his writing better.

• The selections from *Fatherhood* are about being a parent; "Resources on Parenting" on page 59 lists organizations that are helpful to parents with problems or questions.

The selections from *Time Flies* are about aging; "Resources on Aging" on page 61 lists organizations that are helpful to older people with problems or questions.

• This book also has a map on page 46 and a timeline of Bill Cosby's life on page 58.

READING THIS BOOK

If you are a new reader, you may want to have this book or parts of it read aloud to you. Even if you are a more experienced reader, you may enjoy hearing it read aloud before reading it silently to yourself.

Try to be an *active* reader. Here are some things you can do.

Before Reading

• Read the back cover of the book, think about its title and look at the picture on the front. Ask yourself what you expect the book to be about.

• Think about why you want to read the book. Perhaps you want to know what Bill Cosby has to say about parenting or growing older.

• Look at the Contents page. Decide what parts of the book you want to read and in what order you want to read them.

While Reading

• If you come across a word that is difficult to understand, keep reading to see if the meaning becomes clear. If it doesn't, ask someone for the word or look up the word in a dictionary.

• Ask yourself questions while you read. For example, in what ways are Bill Cosby's and my own life similar?

After Reading

• Think about what you have read. Did this book make you think about your own experiences differently?

• Talk with others about what you have read.

The editors of *Writer's Voices* hope you will write to us. We want to know what you think about our books.

About the Selections from
Fatherhood

Bill Cosby wrote his first book, *Fatherhood,* in 1986. In the book, he tells about being the father of five children. The selections we chose from the book describe some of Cosby's experiences with his children: making breakfast for the kids; talking with his teenage son about buying a car; giving directions to a five-year-old who doesn't know left from right.

Cosby's stories are funny; it's easy to tell that they come from his real-life experiences as a father and as a comedian who finds the humor in everyday life. Each story also has a serious message about being a parent and about how parents and children can learn from each other. Cosby seems to be saying that parents need to laugh about their problems with their children, even when they are frustrated or annoyed by them.

Perhaps the selections will remind you

of experiences you've had with your family when you were a child. Or perhaps the selections will remind you of experiences you had with your own children or grandchildren.

Selected from
Fatherhood
BILL COSBY

I am not a psychologist or a sociologist. I do have a doctorate in education, but much more important than my doctorate is my delight in kids. I devote a part of my professional life to entertaining and educating them. I like children. Nothing I've ever done has given me more joys and rewards than being a father to my five. In between these joys and rewards, of course, has come the natural strife of family life, the little tensions and conflicts that are part of trying to bring civilization to children. The more I have talked about such problems, the more I have found that all other parents had the very same ones and are relieved to hear me turning them into laughter.

Yes, every parent knows the source of this laughter. Come share more of it with me now.

Good Morning, Opponents

If a family wants to get through the day with a minimum of noise and open wounds, the parents have to impose order on the domestic scene. And such order should start with breakfast, which we all know is the most important meal of the day. My wife certainly thinks so. A few weeks ago, she woke me at six o'clock in the morning and said, "I want you to go downstairs and cook breakfast for the children."

"But, dear," I said with an incredulous look at the clock, "it's six in the morning."

"You tell time very nicely. Now go down and cook breakfast for the children. They have to go to school."

"But to eat at six . . . isn't that bad for the stomach? I mean, they just ate twelve hours ago."

"Bill, get out of this bed and go downstairs and cook breakfast for your children!"

I would like to repeat a point I made before: I am not the boss of my house. I don't know how I lost it and I don't know where I lost it. I probably never had it to begin with. My wife is the boss, and I do not understand how she is going to outlive me.

"But here's the thing, dear," I said, now a desperate man, "I don't know what they want to eat."

"It's *down* there."

I went back to sleep. I dreamed I was with Scott in the Antarctic, perhaps because my wife was pouring ice water over my head.

"Have you given any more thought to cooking breakfast?" she said as I awoke again.

And so, downstairs I went, wondering about the divorce laws in my state, and I started slamming things around. I had bacon, sausages, and eggs all lined up when my four-year-old arrived, looking so adorable with her cute face and little braids.

"Morning, Daddy," she said.

"Okay," I said, "what do *you* want for breakfast?"

"Chocolate cake," she replied.

"Chocolate *cake*? For *breakfast*? That's ridiculous."

Then, however, I thought about the ingredients in chocolate cake: milk and eggs and wheat, all part of good nutrition.

"You want chocolate cake, honey?" I said, cutting a piece for her. "Well, here it is. But you also need something to drink."

And I gave her a glass of grapefruit juice.

When the other four children came downstairs and saw the four-year-old eating chocolate cake, they wanted the same, of course; and since I wanted good nutrition for them too, I gave each of them a piece.

So there my five children sat, merrily eating chocolate cake for breakfast, occasionally stopping to sing:

Dad is the greatest dad you can make!
For breakfast he gives us chocolate cake!

The party lasted until my wife appeared, staggered slightly, and said, "Chocolate cake for *breakfast*? Where did you all get *that*?"

"*He* gave it to us! *He* made us eat it!" said my five adorable ingrates in one voice; and then my eight-year-old added, "*We* wanted eggs and cereal."

Wheeler-Dealer

Buying a stereo is merely a father's practice for the Big Buy: a car. When his child requests a car, a father will wish that he were a member of some sect that hasn't gone beyond the horse.

"Dad, all my friends say I should have my own car," the boy says earnestly one day.

"Wonderful. When are they going to buy it?"

"No, Dad. They think that you and Mom should buy me the car."

"Is there any particular reason why we should?"

"Well, that's what parents *do*."

"Not *all* parents. Did Adam and Eve get Abel a car? And he was the *good* one. Tell me this: why do you *need* a car?"

"To go places by myself."

"Well, you'd be surprised how many people manage to do that on public transportation. Elderly *ladies* do it every day. It's called a bus and I'd be happy to buy you a token. I won't even wait for your birthday."

"Dad, *you* know a bus isn't cool. My friends say I shouldn't have to ride on a bus now that I'm sixteen."

"They say that? Well, they couldn't be *good* friends because buses are so much fun. They expand your social circle. You meet new people every three blocks."

"That's cute, Dad."

"I know you don't go particularly deep in math, but do you happen to know what a car costs?"

"I'll get a *used* one."

"Terrific. And we'll have a family lottery to try to guess the day it will break down."

"Okay, *slightly* used."

"Which is slightly more or less than five thousand dollars, not counting insurance."

"Insurance?"

"You getting some used insurance too?"

"I'll drive it real carefully."

"And there's a chance you will," you say, suddenly picturing people all over town bouncing off your son's fenders.

"Dad, I just *have* to have a car. Say, what about *yours*? Then you could buy yourself a *new* one. Dad, you *deserve* a new car."

"That's very thoughtful, son," you say, now having heard the ploy you've been expecting.

"Think nothing of it, Dad."

And so, the moment has come for you to gently remind your son precisely how worthless he currently is—without bruising his ego, of course.

"You see," you tell him, "the thing is that unless a wonderful offer came in last night, you have no job. You are sixteen years old, you have no job, and you have an excellent chance of failing the eleventh grade."

"Not *Driver's Ed*! I'm *creaming* that!"

"I'm happy to hear it. You'll go on to college—if we can find one in Baja California—and you'll major in Driver's Ed. Maybe you'll get your M.A. in Toll Booths and even your Ph.D. in Grease and Lube."

"Dad, I wish you wouldn't keep bringing up school. I'm just not motivated."

"To improve your mind, that is. But you *are* motivated to get a car. The bus may not go to the unemployment office."

"Come on, Dad; *you* know what a car means. I need it to *go* places."

"Like a fast-food joint, where your career will be. Because with the grades you have right now, if you somehow *do* happen to be graduated from high school, which the Vatican will declare a miracle, you'll be competing with only ten million others for the job of wrapping cheeseburgers."

"Dad, I'd love to talk more about my career, but I gotta tell you something really exciting that's gonna change your mind: I just saw an ad for a sensational sixty-nine Mustang."

"Really? How much?"

"Just two thousand dollars."

"Just two thousand dollars. Did you happen to ask if it had an engine? And are brakes optional?"

"Dad, I can't understand why you're being so unreasonable."

"That's what fathers are. It's one of the qualifications."

"But my friends keep saying I should *have* a car."

"And they certainly have the right to buy you one. I'll tell you what: how's *this* for reasonable? Bring your friends over here and we'll have a collection, a matching funds collection. Whatever you get from them, I'll match it."

The boy winds up with ninety-six cents.

Remembrance of Things Upstairs

That boy at Lake Tahoe had trouble remembering the address of his school, but he is typical of young people. I have found that children remember only what they want to. It's a talent they develop from the very beginning.

For example, suppose you are sitting in your living room and suddenly realize that you need something from upstairs, but you feel too lazy to make the trip. Luckily, however, you have co-produced a five-year-old who goes upstairs just for fun and who also speaks your language. Morever, at this moment, the child is in your very room, about to destroy an antique.

"Come here," you say to this child and she understands perfectly and moves directly to you. "I want you to get something from my bedroom and bring it down to me."

"*Sure*, Daddy!" the child says, delighted to be honored with such a mission. And this is why you are sending her: because the mission is an honor for her but would do nothing for you.

And now you tell the child not only the exact location of your glasses (on the table to the right of the bed), but also the exact location of your bedroom, as if she has never been in the house before. She is, after all, only five.

Within moments, however, you realize the child is having trouble remembering the difference between the left hand and the right.

"*This* hand," you say. "This hand is the *right* one, okay?"

"If you say so, Daddy."

"I want you to go to the table on Daddy's side of the bed, so here's what you do. Make this hand into a fist, hold it way out, and go upstairs. Leave it balled up in a fist so that when you go through the door, you can go in *its* direction. Won't that be *fun?* As much fun as chocolate cake for breakfast or taking a shower in your clothes. Now you do remember where our bed is, don't you? The one you like to come into when Mommy and I want to be alone."

"Uh-huh."

"Good! So you just go around to the side that's on the same side as your balled-up hand and then go to the table on that side. You know the one with the lamp on it?"

"Uh-huh."

"Well, my glasses are there. Bring Daddy's glasses right down here. Now what did I say?"

"Go upstairs to your room and look on the table," says the child. "With the right hand balled up."

"You are going to do brilliantly on the SATs. Just bring those glasses down to Daddy."

"Okay."

And so, you return to your reading, trying to guess what the words are because your glasses have not yet arrived. After a while, you sense that too much time has passed since you sent the child for the glasses; and then you see this very child walking past your living-room chair, but she says nothing to you. She is simply walking around, so you call her over and say, "Sweetheart, I thought I asked you to get my glasses."

And the sweetheart says, "Oh, yeah. Uh, I didn't see them."

Drawing her closer, you say, "Did you go up to my room?"

"Yeah."

"My room in *this* house?"

"Yeah."

"And you looked on the table?"

"Yeah."

"And you didn't see them?"

"Yeah."

"With your hand balled up?"

"Yeah."

"Okay, now you just go back upstairs and look on that table nice and hard because I know I left them there."

"Well, Dad, I didn't see them. I looked for them and I didn't see them."

"Did you look on the *other* table?"

"No."

At once, you're aware of your own stupidity in not having asked the child to look on both tables. And so, you say to her, "Sweetheart, go up again. Keep your hand balled up on that side and look for the glasses. Keep your *hand* balled up, but nothing else."

And the child goes upstairs again, and this time she comes back, so definite progress has been made.

"They're not there, Dad," she says.

"You definitely looked on the other table?"

"Yeah."

And so you lead the child upstairs.

Both of you have your right hands balled up because this is a learning experience.

"Now we put our hands straight out," you tell her as you enter the bedroom, "and we follow them like this."

And there, on the table, are your glasses.

You start to get angry, but you cannot sustain it, for how can you be angry at a child who is so pretty and biteable? Sustaining anger at a biteable daughter has been a father's timeless problem. I doubt it can ever be solved.

"*Here* are my glasses," you say. "I thought I *told* you they were here."

"But, Dad," she sweetly replies, "they weren't here when I *looked* for them."

"You came over to this side?"

"Yeah."

"And you looked?"

"Yeah."

"And they weren't there?"

"No, Dad. Not there at all."

There are many times during the fathering years when you wonder about the condition of your mind, and this is one of them. I don't think *anyone*, not even a magician or a psychic, could have said whether or not those glasses were on the bedside table when the child went up to look for them. The psychic might have told you, "I see this as a great learning experience."

And she would have been right: you have learned to get your glasses by yourself. Moreover, your child has learned a little something about remembering directions. It may take several more trips to fetch things before her mind will be as well trained as a golden retriever's, but you will keep trying. You will keep trying and keep having patience.

And *that* is fatherhood.

About the Selections from
Time Flies

In 1987, Bill Cosby had his fiftieth birthday. That big day started him thinking about what it means to grow older. These thoughts led him to write his second book, *Time Flies*.

Cosby talks about the changes he sees in himself as he grows older. Although he is funny when he writes about gaining weight or having to wear glasses, it is clear he is not sure he likes these changes. Time flies for everyone, whether you're Bill Cosby or a regular person. Cosby talks about what it means to be 50 years old and how it feels to slow down a little.

The selections from *Time Flies* make the reader laugh and also think. What is "old?" What are some of the good things about aging? Why don't most people like the idea of turning 30? or 40? or 50?

Perhaps these selections will remind

you of experiences you have had dealing with an "important" birthday. Or perhaps they will remind you of changes that you like or don't like in yourself as you grow older.

Selected from
Time Flies
BILL COSBY

Preface: Where To,
Old Cos?

I recently turned fifty, which is young for a tree, mid-life for an elephant, and ancient for a quarter-miler, whose son now says, "Dad, I just can't run the quarter with you anymore unless I bring something to read."

Fifty is a nice number for the states in the Union or for a national speed limit, but it is not a number that I was prepared to have hung on *me*. Fifty is supposed to be my *father's* age, but now Bill Cosby, *Junior*, is stuck with these elevated digits and everything they mean. A few days ago, a friend tried to cheer me up by saying, "Fifty is what forty used to be." He had made an inspirational point; and while I ponder it, my forty-year-old knees are suggesting I sit down and my forty-year-old eyes are looking for their glasses, whose location has been forgotten by my forty-year-old mind.

Am I over the hill? They keep telling me that the hill has been moved, that people are younger than ever. And I keep telling *them* that the high-jump bar has dropped from the six feet five I once easily cleared to the four feet nothing that is a Berlin wall for me now. It is not a pretty sight to see a man jumping a tennis net and going down like something snagged by a lobster fisherman.

"You're not getting older, you're getting better," says Dr. Joyce Brothers. This, however, is the kind of doctor who inspires a second opinion.

And so, as I approach the day when my tennis court jumping will be over the balls (or maybe the lines), I am moved to share some thoughts on aging with you, in case you happen to be getting older too. I am moved to reveal how aging feels to me—physically, mentally, and emotionally. Getting older, of course, is a distinctly better change than the one that brings you eulogies. In fact, a poet named Robert Browning considered it the best change of all:

> Grow old along with me!
> The best is yet to be.

On the days when I need aspirin to get out of bed, Browning is clearly a minor poet; but he was an optimist and there is always comfort in his lines, no matter how much you ache.

Whether or not Browning was right, most of my first fifty years have been golden ones. I have been an exceedingly lucky man, so I will settle for what is ahead being as good as what has gone by. I find myself moving toward what is ahead with a curious blend of both fighting and accepting the aging of Cosby, hoping that the philosopher was right when he said, "Old is always fifteen years from now."

Turning fifty has not bothered me, but

people keep saying it *should* have, for fifty is one of those milestone ages that end in zero. Of course, in America *every* age ending in zero is considered a milestone age. Fifty is called The Big Five-O, but Forty is The Big Four-O and thirty is The Big Three-O. A few months ago, my youngest daughter hit The Big One-O and she wasn't happy about it.

"I wish there were more single figures," she said.

Although reaching this half-century mark has not traumatized me, it *has* left me with disbelief about the flight of time. It seems that only yesterday I was fifteen and old people were people of forty, who were always going someplace to sit down. And now *I* am doing the sitting; and now my wife is telling me, "You *sit* too much. You should get up and *do* something."

"Okay," I say, "let's have some sex."

"Just *sit* there."

When I was eight, an uncle said, "Bill, how long would you like to live?"

"A hundred million years," I replied.

"That's a ripe old age. I wonder what you'll *look* like at a hundred million."

"Oh, I'll just be me," I said.

Now, however, considerably short of the hundred-million mark, I am having to learn to accept a new me, one who has to drink skim milk, which looks like the wash for a paintbrush; one whose stomach refuses to process another jalapeño pepper; and one for whom a lobster is crustacean cyanide.

"If you want a lobster," my doctor says, "just eat the shell."

Have I *also* become just the shell? Well, in one or two places, the meat *is* missing. For example, I am now a man with the ability to dial a telephone number and, while the phone is ringing, forget whom he is calling. Just yesterday, I made such a blind call and a person answered with a voice I did not know. Like a burglar doing research, I quickly hung up, and then I thought about age.

Wiser men than I have thought about age and have never figured out anything to do except say, "Happy birthday." What, after all, *is* old? To a child of seven, ten is old; and to a child of ten, twenty-five is middle-aged and fifty is an archaeological exhibit. And to me, a man of seventy is ... what I want to be, weighing 195, playing tennis with convalescents, and hearing well enough to hear one of my grandchildren sweetly say, "Grandpa, was 'The Cosby Show' anything like 'I Love Lucy'?"

Through a Glass Darkly

I wear glasses, primarily so I can look for the things that I keep losing. One day, however, I did something I do not usually do: I pushed the glasses up to the top of my head when I began to read a magazine because I do not need them for reading. A few minutes later, I put the magazine down, walked out of the office in my house, and went to the kitchen for a glass of lemonade. When I returned to the office, my children were circling my desk like vultures around a dying zebra.

"I would like all of you to please leave Daddy's stuff alone," I told them.

"Don't mind us, Daddy," said my little one. "We're just playing."

"And this is the one place I don't *want* you to play."

"What's this, Daddy?" she said, picking up a script she was planning to shred.

"Your next fifty meals," I replied. "Now go outside and bother your mother. That's what mothers are for."

After they had left, I went back to my reading; but a few minutes later, I decided that I wanted to go to town for some shopping; and so, I put on my jacket, and I also wanted to put on my glasses to drive because part of safe driving is being able to see the other cars.

But where *were* my glasses?

I began to look around my desk, both

in and under things, wondering where my glasses had gone to hide. I checked my cigar humidor and I even checked the big box containing all the things I never use and cannot throw away. The reason I cannot throw them away is simple: some day a friend may call and say, "Do you happen to have any dried-up felt markers? I can't seem to find any in the stores. And do you also happen to have a two-inch pencil with the eraser chewed off? It's my favorite kind."

With a blend of determination and dismay, I now got up and started to walk around the office. I looked like a man who was hunting for Easter eggs.

This does it, I finally thought. *There's no question about it: the kids have definitely taken my glasses. Maybe they need them for the school play. Or maybe they think I'm handsomer without them.*

I did not, however, want to go right in and yell at the kids because such anger in the past had usually triggered the reply, "Of *course* you can't find something. You always leave your stuff lying all *over* the place. The other day there was a can of *insect* spray in the fridge. It had to be yours."

"If people would just leave my stuff where I *put* it," I always say with partial conviction.

I am just like any typical nuclear physicist. My office may look messy, but I know where every atom is.

After brooding about the situation for another few minutes, I suddenly decided that the culprit was not one of my children but my *wife*, who had moved my glasses to a place in our home where they made a better blend with the color scheme. However, greater than my anger at my wife was my desire to do my shopping in town; and so, in one last desperate effort, I searched the living room, the dining room, the kitchen, and even the fuse box.

At last, I went upstairs and searched the bedroom, after which I decided to go into the bathroom for five or ten aspirin. As I entered the bathroom, I caught sight of myself in the mirror; and I also caught sight of something on top of my head: my glasses. They had been resting all this time on the great empty spaces there.

Questions for the Reader

THINKING ABOUT THE STORY

1. What was interesting for you about the selections from *Fatherhood* and *Time Flies*?

2. Did the events or people in the selections become important or special to you in some way? Write about or discuss your answers.

3. What do you think were the most important things Bill Cosby wanted to say in the selections?

4. In what ways did the selections answer the questions you had before you began reading or listening?

5. Were any parts of the selections difficult to understand? If so, you may want to read or listen to them again. Discuss with your learning partners possible reasons why they were difficult.

6. What did you learn about Bill Cosby from reading each selection? If you read the *Fatherhood* selection, how do you think Bill Cosby feels about being a father? If you read the selection from *Time Flies,* how do you think Bill Cosby feels about growing older? Discuss or write about whether you feel the same way or differently than Bill Cosby about being a parent or growing older.

THINKING ABOUT THE WRITING

1. How did Bill Cosby help you see, hear and feel what happened in each selection? Find the words, phrases or sentences that you think did this best.

2. In each selection, Bill Cosby uses dialogue. Dialogue can make a story stronger and more alive. Pick out some dialogue that you feel is strong and explain how it helps the writing.

3. Comedians often take a true experience and exaggerate it to make it funny. Go back to the selections and find any parts where you think Bill Cosby did this.

4. When Bill Cosby writes about himself and his real family, they sound and act a lot like his television character and his television family. You can almost hear Cosby's voice in his writing and you can almost see the people acting and reacting. How does Bill Cosby make you feel that you are right there watching the events in the selections take place?

ACTIVITIES

1. Were there any words that were difficult for you in the selections from *Fatherhood* and *Time Flies*? Go back to these words and try to figure out their meanings. Discuss what you think each word means, and why you made that guess. Look up the words in a dictionary and see if your definitions are the same or different.

Discuss with your learning partners how you are going to remember each word. Some ways to remember words are to put them on file cards, write them in a journal or create a personal dictionary. Be sure to use the words in your writing in a way that will help you to remember their meanings.

2. Talking with other people about what you have read can increase your understanding. Discussion can help you organize your thoughts, get new ideas and rethink your original ideas. Discuss your thoughts about the selections from *Fatherhood* and *Time Flies* with someone else who has read them. Find out if you helped yourselves understand the selections in the same or different ways. Find out if your opinions about the selections are the same or different. See if your thoughts change as a result of this discussion.

3. After you finish reading or listening, you might want to write down your thoughts about the book. You could write your reflections on the book in a journal or you could write about topics the book has brought up that you want to explore further. You could write a book review or a letter to a friend you think might be interested in the book.

4. Did reading the selections give you any ideas for your own writing? You might want to write about:

• Your own experience of being a parent or grandparent.

• A humorous event from your own childhood.

• How you feel about growing older.

• An event that made you realize how getting older affected you.

5. Sometimes organizing information in a visual way can help you better understand or remember it. Look at the timeline for Bill Cosby on page 58. You might want to make a similar timeline for your own life.

6. If you are a fan of *The Cosby Show* or any other situation comedy, watch a few episodes and focus on the characters. Make a list of each character's special traits that always get a laugh. For example, the character could be sloppy or obnoxious, old-fashioned or always hungry. Think about this list and when you do your own writing, try to give each person special personality traits that make him or her unique.

7. You could do research on the larger role that fathers are taking today in raising their children. Or you could do some additional reading about the topic of aging. You could use what you learn to make a presentation to your learning partners. Part of your research might be to interview someone who knows about these topics.

8. If you could talk to Bill Cosby, what questions would you ask him about his writing? You might want to write the questions in a journal.

Map of Places Mentioned in This Book

MASSACHUSETTS

Philadelphia

New York City

Los Angeles/ Beverly Hills

ATLANTIC OCEAN

CARIBBEAN SEA

N

About Bill Cosby

Bill Cosby's Childhood and Teenage Years

Bill Cosby was born near Philadelphia, Pennsylvania, on July 12, 1937. His parents named him William Henry Cosby, Junior.

His father was in the Navy, so he was away from home a lot. His mother, Anna, worked as a housekeeper. They lived in a housing project in North Philadelphia.

Cosby has two brothers, Russell and Robert. He had another brother, James, who died when he was young. Bill Cosby was the oldest.

As a child, Cosby loved playing sports. He says in his book, *Time Flies*, "The boys and I played baseball, basketball, football, and stickball for eight or nine hours with no breaks.... On summer nights, we often played until it got dark—and then we played more."

Bill Cosby has always loved to be funny. He liked to make his friends laugh.

He spent a lot of time making up jokes and telling them to his family and friends.

In 1956, Cosby joined the Navy. He spent four years in the Navy, working in a hospital unit. The hospital unit traveled up and down the Atlantic Coast and the Caribbean. When he was in the Navy, he had time to play sports. He won many track and field events.

Bill Cosby's Education

Bill Cosby realized that he wanted to go back to school while he was in the Navy. He studied hard and passed the test for a high school equivalency diploma.

When he got out of the Navy, Cosby got an athletic scholarship to Temple University. Temple University is in Philadelphia. He won three varsity letters at Temple. He was a runner and a high jumper.

Bill Cosby started out in college to be a teacher. He has always placed a very high value on education. He thought that, in his career, he would try to help children learn.

To help pay for school, he got a job as a bartender. The owner of the bar gave him the chance to do comedy routines for his customers. The customers liked his jokes.

Cosby decided to take a chance and see if he could become a successful comedian. During a school vacation in 1962, he went to New York City. He got booked into a nightclub. The customers in New York City liked his jokes too.

An agent saw Cosby at the New York City nightclub and signed him up. Soon, the agent got him a club date in Chicago, Illinois.

Now, Cosby had to make a hard decision. Should he continue in school, or should he start a career in show business? He decided to leave school a second time. He decided to try to make it as a comedian.

Bill Cosby writes about making this

decision. He says, in his book, *Time Flies*, "Although my mother and father kept telling me that I should finish college before I flopped in show business, I felt that only *I* ... knew what was best for me."

Cosby learned a lesson from his decision to drop out of college. In *Time Flies*, he says he has told his own children that "they should finish their formal education and then go on to be what they wanted to be."

In the early 1970s, Bill Cosby decided that he wanted to go back to college and finish. His parents had always been sorry that he hadn't finished college. Cosby, himself, had never forgotten that he had an unfinished goal. And he also wanted to learn more about teaching children.

Bill Cosby and his family moved from Beverly Hills, California to Massachusetts so he could go to school at the University of Massachusetts. In 1977, at the age of 39, he received a Ph.D. in education.

Bill Cosby's Career

Once Bill Cosby decided to try a career as a comedian, he started getting more and more club dates all over the country.

Cosby got a break when he was asked to be on the television program, *The Tonight Show*. He was a hit and his career took off.

In 1965, Bill Cosby got another break. He was cast as the co-star, with Robert Culp, of a new television show called *I Spy*. Cosby played the part of a secret agent named Alexander Scott. The show was a big success and was on television for three years.

When *I Spy* went off television, Cosby began to work on his own television series. It was called *The Bill Cosby Show*. He played the part of a high school teacher and track coach named Chet Kincaid. The show went on television in September 1969 and ran until August 1971.

Bill Cosby had taken a chance when

he decided to make it as a comedian. Now that he was a big success, he would work on his old dream of helping children to learn.

In 1971, he started working on a new television show called *The Electric Company*. This show was for children. It taught them about reading in an entertaining way. This show was on television for five years.

At the same time, Cosby put together a cartoon television show called *Fat Albert and the Cosby Kids*. Bill Cosby narrated the show and he also was the voice of Fat Albert and some of the other characters. Cosby wanted this show to teach children reading, writing, and arithmetic. He also wanted it to teach good behavior and good values. Cosby got a team of experts to help him make sure the show lived up to his goals.

Fat Albert and the Cosby Kids was very popular, both with children and their parents. Bill Cosby understood how to make children laugh and how to make them learn while they were laughing.

In 1971, Bill Cosby began to star in movies. He made one movie almost every year for over ten years. His best-known movies are *Uptown Saturday Night* and *Let's Do It Again.* Cosby co-starred in these movies with Sidney Poitier.

In 1983, he made a movie called *Bill Cosby Himself.* He was not only the star but also the writer and the director.

Almost everything Bill Cosby did was a success. His biggest setback was a television show called *Cos.* It went on television in September 1976 and was cancelled in October. The show's biggest problem was competition from popular programs that were on at the same time.

It was a long time before Bill Cosby tried to do another television show. Then he got the idea of a show about a doctor, his wife, and their children. It would be funny, but it would also be true to life. But the most important thing about the show would be the way it showed good family values. The name of the show would be *The Cosby Show*. And Bill Cosby would play the part of the doctor whose name would be Heathcliff Huxtable.

Bill Cosby had another idea for this show. It would be filmed in New York City. This was unusual since most shows are made in Los Angeles, California.

The Cosby Show went on television in September 1984. It was the number one show that year. The final episode was broadcast on April 30, 1992. Now in reruns, it is still one of the most popular shows on television.

Bill Cosby does much more than make television shows. He makes commercials. He makes personal appearances. And he writes books.

Bill Cosby's Family

While Cosby was performing at a club in Washington, D.C., he met Camille Hanks. She was in college at the University of Maryland. On January 25, 1964, they got married.

Camille and Bill Cosby have five children: Erika Ranee, born in 1965; Erinn Chalene, born in 1966; Ennis William, born in 1969; Ensa Camille, born in 1975; and Evin Harrah, born in 1977.

With five children of his own, Bill Cosby has a lot of experience in raising children. As he says in his book, *Fatherhood*, "Child raising is still a dark continent and no one really knows anything. You just need a lot of love and luck."

For much of the biographical material on Bill Cosby, we have relied on Bill Adler's *The Cosby Wit* (New York, 1986), as well as *Contemporary Authors* (Detroit, 1979) and *Contemporary Theatre, Film, and Television* (Detroit, 1986).

Bill Cosby with some members of his TV family on *The Cosby Show*. (Courtesy AP/Wide World Photos.)

Bill Cosby and his
wife, Camille, at
a party in 1966.
(Courtesy AP/Wide
World Photos.)

Bill Cosby in 1969 doing a stand-up comedy
act about one of his most famous characters,
Fat Albert. (Courtesy AP/Wide World Photos.)

A Timeline for Bill Cosby

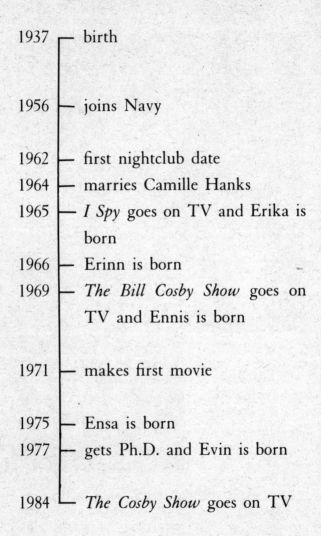

1937	birth
1956	joins Navy
1962	first nightclub date
1964	marries Camille Hanks
1965	*I Spy* goes on TV and Erika is born
1966	Erinn is born
1969	*The Bill Cosby Show* goes on TV and Ennis is born
1971	makes first movie
1975	Ensa is born
1977	gets Ph.D. and Evin is born
1984	*The Cosby Show* goes on TV

Resources on Parenting and Aging

PARENTING

A good source of classes on parenting, classes you can take with your children or after-school programs for your kids is your local YMCA, YWCA or YMHA. Look in your local phone book for listings.

If you're expecting a child, you can call your local hospital or health clinic to see if they have classes for expectant or new parents.

Organizations you can call for help or information

Families Anonymous
P.O. Box 3475
Culver City, CA 90231-3475
800-736-9805
Self-help organization for friends and relatives concerned about the use of drugs or alcohol by children or adults.

Family Service America
11700 West Lake Park Drive
Milwaukee, WI 53224
414-359-1040
Federation of agencies providing family counseling and other programs to help families with parent-child, marital, mental health and other probems of family living.

National Foster Parents Association
9 Dartmoor Drive
Crystal Lake, IL 60014
815-455-2527
Advocacy group whose members are foster parents,
social workers and others interested in enhancing the
role of foster parenting. Publishes reports, pamphlets
and other materials.

**National PTA-National Congress of Parents
and Teachers**
330 N. Wabash Avenue
Chicago, IL 60611-3690
312-670-6782
Works for legislation to benefit young people and
contributes materials on parent education, adolescent
sexuality and TV and its effects on children. If you want
to be more involved in your child's school, check your
local phone book for the number of the Parent-Teacher
Association.

Parent Cooperative Pre-Schools International
P.O. Box 90410
Indianapolis, IN 46290-1040
317-849-0992
Individuals and groups interested in preschool education
in nonprofit nursery schools operated by parents on a
cooperative basis.

Parents Without Partners
401 N. Michigan Avenue
Chicago, IL 60611-4267
800-637-7974 or look in your local phone book
Promotes acceptance of single parenting. Provides
information and support services for single parents.

Step Family Foundation
333 West End Avenue
New York, NY 10023
800-759-7837 or 212-744-6924
Counsels and provides information to people in step
situations.

Toughlove, International
P.O. Box 1069
Doylestown, PA 18901
800-333-1069
Support groups for parents of problem teenagers.

AGING

Many states and counties have Offices for the
Aging. These are a good source of information
on programs and resources. Check your local telephone book or directory assistance for a listing.

You may wish to see if there is a Foster

Grandparents Program in your area. Volunteer seniors work on a one-to-one basis with children who have special needs.

Organizations you can call for help or information

Alzheimer's Association
919 N. Michigan Avenue, Suite 1000
Chicago, IL 60611
800-621-0379
Information for family members of sufferers from Alzheimer's disease (a brain disease common in the elderly causing memory loss and other changes in personality and behavior).

American Association of Retired Persons
601 E Street NW
Washington, DC 20049
202-434-2277
Membership open to people 50 years old or older, whether retired or employed. Focuses on improving every aspect of living for older people. Offers group health insurance, travel information, etc.

Children of Aging Parents
1609 Woodburn Road, Suite 302A
Levittown, PA 19057
800-227-7294
Self-help organization for the education and support of caregivers to the elderly.

Elderhostel, Inc.
75 Federal Street
Boston, MA 02110-1941.
617-426-7788
Offers low-cost, short-term residential academic
programs at schools and universities for adults 60 years
of age and over. Provides financial aid. Free catalog of
classes available.

Gray Panthers
2025 Pennsylvania Avenue NW, Suite 819
Washington, DC 20006
800-280-5362
Works to combat discrimination on the basis of age;
maintains information and referral service.

National Caucus and Center for Black Aged
1424 K Street NW, Suite 500
Washington DC 20005
202-637-8400
Information and referral service.

National Council on the Aging
409 3rd Street SW, Suite 200
Washington, DC 20024
202-479-1200
National information and consultation center for
programs for the elderly.

National Council of Senior Citizens
1331 F Street, NW
Washington, DC 20004
202-347-8800
Education and action group that supports programs to aid
senior citizens.